Heterotopia

Heterotopia

Lesley Wheeler

Barrow Street Press
New York City

Designed by Robert Drummond

Cover photo:
    Reflections Photo Archive,
    20thcenturyimages.co.uk

Author photo by David Peterson

Published by Barrow Street Press
Distributed by:
    Barrow Street
    P.O. Box 1831
    Murray Hill Station
    New York, NY 10156

First Edition

Library of Congress control number: 2010928379

ISBN 978-09819876-2-0

For my mother, Patricia Wheeler,
and my daughter, Madeleine Wheeler Gavaler

CONTENTS

Elsewhere

Forged

When she says stove she means fireplace,
a great soot-blackened maw. When I say
Liverpool I mean an unreal city, purified
of reeking detail like a fairy tale

or a film set, rotted and peeling
like cheap furniture handed down. A girl
might safely climb into the leaping
flames, now rinsed and mythical,

cooled by duplication. I cannot
even place the telling—whether
in a kitchen I could strew with tokens
of work and talk, daughter and mother

crying over onions, or in some moving
car. My memories of her memories
too alloyed. I can only give them
to the fire, piece by broken piece.

Here is mold to flourish on damp walls.
Here the scuff, bang of stout shoes
against some table leg. Here the appalled
lumps of boiled vegetables, formerly rose

and jade and carroty-gold. Someone's tenor
cry, the smell of wool that never dries.
This blitzed, hungry, smoke-thin world
invented me, and its ardent lies

are my birthright. Some history may
be true. Even mine. She was born.
The sun was warm, and the news it made
discovered by coal as it burns.

Heterotopia

Liverpool is at the present moment the center of consciousness of the human universe.
—Allen Ginsberg, 1965

Dame Liverpool has, swathed in flowing white robe and candle in hand cried Mea Maxima Culpa! The penance has been protracted, and not only in absolution long over-due, but I suggest that instead of wearing the penitent's garb any longer she, on the other hand, might well don the wreath of victory; for, thanks to the Liverpool School of Tropical Medicine, the lives of millions of negroes have been saved. Dame Liverpool sinned, suffered, and in our own day has made ample and generous restitution.
—J.H. Dow, 1927

London will be our historic city—the city of culture, fashion, and intellect. But whoever lives long enough will find the great city on the banks of the Mersey will be the commercial city of the future.
—The Liverpool Magazine, 1890

There is not a brick in your dirty town but what is cemented by the blood of a negro.
—attributed to George Cook, 1772

1.
anywhere I sleep is the scene and tonight
I crash in Brian Patten's Toxteth flat—
the University don't care that
Ginsberg chants in the box room by moonlight,
Buddhist things—I helped him with the washing
up when he moved to Henri's Canning Street place,
beard unfurled—what about consciousness,
Liverpool the center of, you're wondering:
yeah, the Beatles were Angels, and Lennon a sexy
longhair raising up his joyful voice
"in electric Afric hurrah"—loving, boys,
is the only redemption—climb into my taxi
and I'll show you the way, a moment's vision aglow
in the mirror, the Cavern the cellars the holds below

2.
Look down, one world inside the next.
Warehouse, museum, glass
display case, and the smallest box:
a diorama Derby House

where doll-size Wrens push ladders about,
thumb pushpins into maps.
Here in the "Dungeon" they fight the real war.
An analyst dreams in the gaps

between transmissions from the Enigma
cipher machine. She believes
the Brits will win, that tacks are U-boats,
that seven feet of concrete

means she's safe. She knows her brother
bunks in a distant convoy,
unsleeping yet alive, hating
the stink of the sailor above,

the shift of the ocean beneath. History
is small and far away
but it was then too, just as I
am small and far away to you.

3.
Enter with Alexandre Promio and you encounter a lamppost
in some two-tone windup industrial Narnia, St. George's Hall
tilting back its toothy head in approval. No one but you is lost:

vans hustle by with their elbows out and dryad men, full
of mutton and commerce, stomp through in gray overcoats.
Welcome to Lime Street in 1896, filmed on the diagonal—

the Brothers Lumière sought the effect of depth. Sunlight Soap,
sings the horse-drawn trolley, before the billboard glints
and turns the corner. Nestlé Milk, another sign coaxes,

while the cinématographe cranks round. Promotions in print
roll and pitch through the sixteen frames per second, because this
city is all business, as is Promio the cameraman, who squints

through his lenses at a new industry. Welcome to the movies,
the quays shot from the Overhead Railway, the immoral river.
Sails furled, the masts will remind you of burnt forests. Past Princes

Dock, lumberyards. In six surviving minutes, brightness stirs
mainly in steam ghosts that haunt the flanks of boats;
wakes scrawled in chains across the water; and in the words.

4.
From Liverpool with brass, textiles, guns
        to the Bight of Biafra. Canny traders
                check the bolts of cloth, taste
the watered-down whiskey,
        and then stack the hull's plank beds
                with people. The coastal forts
stock a good supply. Six weeks to Jamaica
        if the winds are fair—most of the cargo will
                endure the pestilent hold, the stench
and starvation, to raise sugar and
        New World tobacco and fill the ships
                again. It takes trust to buy and sell
anyone: sons sent to learn business
        in England; intermarriage; letters
                of reference inscribed on ivory
bands; a name known along the coast for
        generations. Without this social
                capital, there is only human
collateral, a daughter held in
        pawn, working for the creditor, till
                the debt be repaid or finally
forfeit, and she becomes one of the
        twenty-five thousand Africans per
                year on board a Liverpudlian
slaving ship. The end of the eighteenth
        century. More than two million pounds
                invested. The numbers fade before
one woman bound to one beam. When she
        refuses to eat, sailors force-feed
                her handfuls of rice and yams. One bored
crew member rapes her by starlight. She
        is alone in her language, her thirst,
                her dysentery. An other place.

5.
heterotopia: enables utopia elsewhere (slave trade); physical
and fantasmatic, the room one glimpses in a mirror (an idea of
a city derived from stories); sediment of meaning (ill-drained
marshlands, low cliffs of glacial till); in a real place several
impossible sites are juxtaposed; whenever I need an elsewhere
(boarding school/honeymoon/prison); slices of time
preserved (museum, library); steamship (no civilization
without boats)

6.
I have no right to write,
no visa to any clouded
country. A poem
is a heterotopia
of citizenship: these
are my papers, counterfeit.
My countrywomen
are characters. I vote
in an obscure district.
I step through the glass
and leave white fingerprints
on the frame. I am sorry
for breaking things. I am
glad it is not real
to me. An accent
sounds like, but is not
really, a place to live.

Concerning the Līver Bird

(lī ' ver) [A back-formation from the name *Liverpool*.] *A name arbitrarily given to the bird figured in the arms of the city of Liverpool.*

I.
Eighteen feet high with a twelve-foot wingspan, one of a
         copper pair above the Mersey, erected 1910, copied on
         football jerseys,
my liver bird towers like a cormorant, gleaming fisher of the
         intertidal mudflats, with "laver" or seaweed streaming
         from its noble beak.
The seaweed may once have been broom, emblematic of the
         Plantagenets.
Or it may have been a child, Ganymede, future cupbearer to
         Zeus, ferried up to Olympus by an eagle.
The city seal, destroyed in the siege of 1644, once displayed
         the eagle of King John.
The new designer had never seen an eagle and did not know
         it carried prey in its talons, or he wasn't as deft as the
         old artist, or he was bored and manufacturing trouble.
Ergo, the duck with something nasty in its bill.

II.
Not the barnacle goose, that grows on a tree,
nor the giant roc carrying elephants home to feed its
         hatchlings,
nor caladrius averting its eyes from imminent death,
nor the bird of paradise, brooding midair on the back of its
         mate as it flies toward the sun until it drops,
nor the irritable phoenix plotting immolation in its ball of
         myrrh,
nor the martyr avalerions, who drown themselves when the
         chicks hatch,
for my emblem.

The ancient Britons, those mythical birds,
called the place *llethr-pwll,* or *slope by the stream.*

Perhaps they trained cormorants to dive for fish.
Perhaps one day, long before liver birds,
a few women perched on some rocks
to delouse their squirming children,
exclaim at a naughty tattoo,
enjoy a bit of sunshine before the climate changed.
Imagine the light bending over the estuary,
flickering in coppery golds and greens,
while the air in their mouths tasted of salt,
and a sweet-voiced mother began to sing.

Mr. Hawthorne Peeks at Me Shelf Kit, c. 1854

Some of them sit on the doorsteps, nursing their unwashed babies at bosoms which we will glance aside from, for the sake of our mothers and all womanhood, because the fairest spectacle is here the foulest.
    –Nathaniel Hawthorne, *Our Old Home*

Handsome, yes, the new Consul,
with thirsty eyes and a gloom of curls.
They say he broods all day beneath
the Goose and the Gridiron, giving alms
to them as don't deserve it, scoundrels
and sailors with broken heads, if
he isn't milking the daylight over books
at Henry Young's. Mind, he's punctual
enough at the baker's every noon,
stuffing his gob for tuppence with hot
buns and butter. Not pining away
for America, is he? For some it's gin
from an old shaving mug at the spirit-
vault—for him it's pacing Tithebarn
Street, watching mams belt children
or hawk a bit of hungry cheese.
There he goes, peeping at my bosom
and away again quick, stumbling
and clutching his guilty heart.

It's snowing flakes of coal today.
They catch in my baby's hair and glitter
there, rags of sunshine on the Mersey.
She's a pretty thing, too thin, but wise
enough to keep her lashes low.
Nothing to see, is there, but the empty
shopwindows and the cellar doors
agape. Different ways of looking famished.

Poem without a Landscape

Virginia does not care for me.
The volunteer tomatoes, unlike the kettle song,
do not climb and fatten. A rackety storm
smashes the sunflowers. August bleaches
the protest on the bumper stickers.

New Jersey does not miss me.
Inchworms unspool their veils
between the Dutch roofs and the parkway.
Those bead curtains, unlike the toothy pages
of my books, do not breeze open.
Wild onions taste of homesickness.

Liverpool does not recognize me.
Smoke of a million Woodbines glitters
in the raindrops. The cathedral my grandfather
built for the faithless exhales a rusty sigh.
The pavement, unlike a bad idea,
won't break for scraps of living ground.
The damp air speaks in Scouse.

I don't mind that it rinses my print away.
My fathers are sailors—the fathers on paper.
Who knows what other men swam those private beaches
while the women waited one year, maybe two?
My mother sailed, too. The land is not my mother.
It minds its own business, and welcome to it.
You can see the hills brooding on their own blues.
I'll be my green world—it can seethe inside of me.

Twilight Sleep

Stop up the keyholes and draw the shades.
Awakening is touching a candle-
wick with a match-tip: a burning smell,
some flickering light, the little roar
of chemistry. You cannot remember it later.

Some woman long ago drank caudle, laboring
in a dim room, stroked by a midwife. Forgotten.
Even my great-grandmother's suffering
was never told, save for the last birth, seventeen
years after the rest. *Go to the pictures,*
Father said, and the elder children grabbed
the coins and ran. They didn't know and he
was ashamed. The newborn small and powerful,
distilled from the ether, dreams, old rain.

My mother's dress was pressed, her lipstick
pink. My Brylcreemed father drove her around
and around the block until midnight passed,
evading the charge for an extra day.
The nurses strapped her down and hours
of pain vaporized—she did not believe,
in the morning, that I had been born. Who
is that dark girl, her eyes like the first mud,
effervescing. A stranger, a to-do list.

Books say there are good births, but I
don't believe it. All beginnings hurt
someone: the animal, the ground. So much
to witness and all of it slipping away.

Unlock the cupboards, lift all the lids
in the house, to open the womb. Cast rushes
on the floor and heat milk for bathing. Touch
honey to the infant's tongue to wake her hunger,
to sweeten her voice, for she is thinking even
now about the darkness and how to say it.

Inland Song

In some kind houses the doors
never quite shut. Every table
hosts a bowl of eggs—wooden ones
or striped stone, cool to touch.

What could grow in such an egg?
A day becomes a story becomes a bird,
a lost seagull who shrinks each time
I describe him. Watch him fold

his filigree wings, crawl into
the shell. His song wasn't much,
but he tries to swallow it,
as if he can retreat

to an ornamental state
of potential. This is not possible,
even in an inland village named
Barnacle. Just brush your fingers

over the eggs as you leave,
memorize the feel of the grain.
The paths are thick with nettles,
but if they sting, rub the blisters

with a fistful of dock. Pain
and consolation grow next
to each other, in some kind
countries. House and wing.

Vronhill Street in Liverpool 8

1.

I'm sorry for you, he tells me over a breakfast
bap. I remove the black pudding from my roll—
a shiny disc of blood—and give it to
my uncle, a kind and hospitable man.
Mine was the last generation of Anglo-Saxons
to rule, to know the world belonged to us.

His car had halted everywhere from the Albert
Dock to Dingle, but blasted through Toxteth at speed.
These roads are dangerous now, the foreign-
born drivers. I'm telling this backward. He must have been
afraid to stop until we reached the park,
its clean café with china mugs of tea.

2.
Liverpool 8 means riots to most. Petrol
bombs and paving stones, 1981.
Somalis and Caribbeans had colonized
the terraced houses. The police planted
drugs on the men, called it "agriculture."
Five hundred arrested, a thousand officers
injured, a hundred buildings destroyed. Nine days.
Tear gas. The copper dome of the Rialto
was lit from inside by the flames. A beacon
for some perilous crossing, pulsing. A witness.

3.

After the war, we lived on Vronhill Street,
somewhere off to the right. That's been razed
since. Erwin's, the grocer, was on that corner.
Our landlady in that house, she offered me
three p to drown a bunch of kittens. A lot
of money it was to me. Yes, Vronhill
might be Welsh. All the construction was Welsh
around here, pale brick houses too close together,
no sanitation, shared privies round the back.

4.
Liverpool didn't make the Domesday
Book, but Toxteth did as Stochestede,
the stockaded place. It could be a Viking
word—where Toki planted his staith, marking
a settlement. There was a Roman road
along the Otterspool end, a cache of coins
found and lost again, but the caesars judged
this bit of land not worth a fort and stayed
in Chester. An estuary, too boggy. The Anglo-
Saxons, like the Romans, couldn't be bothered.

King John mapped out the Royal and Ancient Park
of Toxteth for his deer, an inky patch
of parchment that was chartered back and forth
for centuries. Only scraps remained green.
Where slavers had docked, the starving Irish landed,
to be housed in the city's most fetid streets.
Life expectancy seventeen years.

5.

Only a few carved stones and axe-heads
survive from Neolithic Toxteth. Chop
it down, clear the ground, and start again.

He remembers nibble by crumb, as I record
the gardenless yards, every sky a dirty
blank. Even my uncle is a tourist now—
he moved to London many losses ago.

If I had a family tree, it would
be pocked and charred but rooted here, on a street
that no longer exists. Skeptical birds
would haunt its limbs, cackling at the very
idea that anyone owns anything:
*We may sing your name by accident, a nonsense
sound—do not make too much of it.*
The branches would forget where their feet
were buried, and every leaf would document
an imaginary history. I'd belong
to it whether it wanted me or not.

The Calderstones

The Calderstones

1

Six sandstone megaliths slouch in a ruddy ring,
almost forgotten, veiled by weeds, housed
behind some misty glass. Just look at the things:
they yearn to loom awesomely, but cows
have chafed their shabby hides on them, cascades
of soot have discolored them, and resting men
have traced their bootsoles there with worn-down blades.
These rocks, older than the hulks at Stonehenge,
once braced a burial chamber hexed by loops,
cups, spirals, arcs. They lost their first site that lanes
could be widened. The mound itself was scooped
up as fertilizer. Liverpool shrugs and shrines
topple—are built again as a hobbyist's quirk.
It was a mistake to arrange them in circle.

2

Merseyside is all mistakes and circles.
Its rumpled parks are cut from manor lands sold
to a chain of merchants. The slave-trade triangle—
from Liverpool to Africa with cloth in the hold,
to the Americas with human beings, and home
again with cotton for the mills—had folded
and the money was spinning away by the time
the city conceived these antidotes to squalid
housing, these gardens, once woods and pleasure
grounds for the titled, and before that wild terrain
for hunters and gatherers. What would there
be to forage for now among rhododendrons
and other ornamental plants? Nothing
to eat, nowhere to go, pretty paths weaving.

3

Nothing to eat, nowhere to go, and the day
is underbrewed, like tea in cool water,
but the four children set out anyway,
warned to keep out of the kitchen till supper-
time at least. Obedient, empty-pocketed,
they file through Prince's Park to Sefton Park,
where the eldest two scatter in the thickets.
The loyal girl sucks on the brush of one dark
plait, plotting, grasping her little brother's hand.
Perhaps the kind of children who can afford
to lose a toy will be sailing boats. Those are grand
to watch. The blitzed Palm House is boarded
up, though, and she wouldn't give her bread to a swan,
if she had any. Summer is hungry and long.

4

Near the end of summer, the hungry girl
rides three city buses to her new school
by Calderstones Park. Crumbs of fog whirl
around the gate, where three young statues
of the Seasons pose next to the hag Winter.
The trees beyond them shed their hair,
sprout it again, shudder in August thunder-
storms, and blaze golden, years spinning faster
and faster, flickering, decayed, unstable.
She disembarks, spots two more uniforms
and a mum in furs. "You there," the lady whistles,
"and you, meet my daughter. What are your names?
You're going to be friends." The girls smile, link
arms, sally off, leave the old woman shivering.

5

The trembling crone who managed Calder High
did not want the scholarship girls. All twenty,
presto, sequestered in the tower, mind
and matter, to study math, religion, history
before and after their beans and spotted dick.
They played lacrosse—less damage to the sod
than hockey—and rode buses to the Philharmonic,
St. George's Hall, the Walker, to be dosed
with Art like castor oil. Most urgently,
each apprentice practiced elocution, so
she would not sound Liverpudlian. A "t"
evicted the "r" at the end of "wha," no
"ayes" survived, and any judy with sense
would lift her scoured face and apply the past tense.

6

The past tense could shelve the war but not the scoured
roads, the skeleton homes, the rationing that marred
her fifties girlhood. Ask my mother now
and soon she recalls two ounces of sugar,
the cup of orange juice on Fridays at school
to save the poor children from scurvy, milky
puddings, pies on Sundays, trying to choose
the tiniest candies at the sweetshop. See
her find in her Christmas stocking, just once, a ripe
and freckly banana. On the table, just once,
a roast bird, horribly like the chickens
in her books. Then every slop and scrap
into the pigswill bins. The rag-and-bone man
cries for the rest, forlorn in his wagon.

7

"Anny ur-gar, bols, buns," the rag-and-bone man spat.
The salt man, too, with barrow or horse, came
in an old brown coat that their turnips and fat
might have some savor. He lived in the same
briny town and knew how tears preserve the dead,
how money is stained with sweat, how bland are the roots
that fatten underground. Salt can be mined
from caves in the Dungeon south of Liverpool
or evaporated from the tidal waters,
but three pounds of coal must burn for one pound
of salt to be boiled from the sea. Teach your daughters,
translate for your sons. It's an incoherent sound,
the shout of the unshaven man in the dirty cap,
but he has what you need and he sells it cheap.

8

If he has what you need it won't be cheap, so send
your canniest child to the greengrocer and tell
him to wait till the shop is empty. It's your job to tend
five starving bodies, and the coupons will not fill
them. Some black-market potatoes might stretch a bit
of meat a little further, some carrots, leeks,
or any wilted starchy roots that wait
beneath the counter. You feed them all, some weeks,
but put yourself to bed with a mug of hot
water and an Oxo cube. When your wild girl throws
the scouse out the window, pretending that the dog
has been sick, or when your melt-eyed boy who knows
better mixes the sugar, salt, and pepper, it
becomes your duty to beat them into appetites.

9

It was a man's duty to shelter his beaten-down
sister and her two teenage boys, although
how six people in three beds could make room
for three more was anybody's guess. She'd go
soon, he promised, but everyone else in the clan
had put them up before, and this time they closed
their lace curtains: never again. Their aunt was good fun,
the kids decided. Little sums disappeared,
and trinkets from the cabinets, but then
she burst in with sacks of cream buns. That generous,
she was, and full of comic stories. Well, one
green dawn his wife's engagement ring was missed.
Pawned, and no money to buy it back with. Gone,
the emerald hour. Auntie homeless again.

10

Lately the water is diamond-hatched, home again
to salmon, that once was the foulest river in Europe,
or near enough. Conceived in the peaks, it ends
in a salty bay. The silt constricts its hope—
its girth keeps shrinking and now it cannot float
great ships. Ferries, though, have troubled
it for nearly a thousand years: monks who rowed
by hand, sailing ships, paddle steamers. Rabble
in thousands crossed from Liverpool for stunted
holidays on New Brighton Beach. Most could not
afford swimsuits, and it was cold. They huddled
on the strand in their shifts and sleeves, brewing pots
of tea on smoking coals. The wind had no mercy.
Grand liners puffed by on the hardworking Mersey.

11

A hardworking man makes no shift for grand notions
like hospital care. A rodent ulcer nibbled at
his face for years till he collapsed. The ocean
flowed to meet his furious current. That
clash would have finished him, the electrician's mate
shorted out, but a nurse pulled his wife aside.
"The doctors are starving him," she hissed. Eyes met.
My grandmother brought him home, where he died
more slowly. She emptied bedpans, washed his sheets,
worked in the pawnshop, kept her father's books.
Their teenagers paid the rent. He had a neat
memory for poems before the strokes took.
"The boy stood on the burning deck," he'd declare,
ere they all sank, ennobled, into the fire.

12

Those Tom Mix movies have lapsed into flames since—
they were filmed on combustible nitrate stock—
but my mother used to scam sixpence
off my aunt for ice cream and ride shanks'
pony to the Rialto to see him. Always a newsreel,
then a cartoon, and finally the cowboys: John
Wayne, Hopalong, the Lone Ranger. Some shine still,
those drawling galoots with sunburns and guns,
spinning so fast over the beam that they seem
alive. She vanishes after them, into the sunset.
On a red-eye, I return, my boots agleam
with cactus spines. I'll glance around, jump a jet
back west in a wink—who could bear the damp?—
it's like the whole bleak town is an exit ramp.

13

Missing the exit, my uncle steers to the right,
looping round and round the ring road. The tour
is slower than we expected, streets changed, backseat
choked with carsick children. We snap pictures
of ancestral houses, slight and decrepit though adorned
for the World Cup, and suck on humbugs. "That's
where Matthew Arnold snuffed it, dashing for
a wooden tram. It made me sick how they pitched.
Once my neighbor said, 'A tomato's good
for that,' and the thought of those jelly seeds, God,
I never forgave her. Can't bear tomatoes even
now." The imagination works that way. A strong
emotion juiced with texture or a scent is better
than a memory: rosier, tarter, wetter.

14

He has a red memory of the Calderstones,
a stone circle in the rain, no, under glass,
and quizzes the locals til we find them. Some
recollections have bones, gritty mass
that you could touch if they would let you. Others
are thin, a fog on the river that a prow
might cut through, only to perish or blur
again. Under those clouds, sandstone shows
everywhere: the back stoops, grooved from whetting
knives; the blushing cathedral, gothic on steroids;
the cliffs and banks washed bald in cold floods;
the sedimentary language we speak together;
and here, before us in untidy brush, where
six sandstone megaliths slouch in a ruddy ring.

Legends

Widdershins

The year turns in reverse, nature
unsaying her own hard words.

Low dirty snowbanks strive
to remember lightness. Puffed
with nostalgia, they shrug off
the soot, divide into crystal
particles. Flakes leap
skyward. Ripe clouds inhale
them, dissolve into wisps.
Leaves jump, flushing,
onto wet branch-hooks.

Look up at the green fruit
withdrawing from your hand,
shrinking as spring
yanks up its lacy knickers.
Will the petals back
into cool sheaths, your own
fleshy decades receding
into airy notions. Watch
the tree skin grow thin
as your grandmother's words spin
into a high pure cry. Every
pitch that roughened and fell
can rise again. Stories can,
with a damp sigh,
dissipate into sense.

Split, 1940

She gave birth   to her third
child on a   coal-sooted
kitchen floor.   Soldiers and

sailors thronged   Merseyside
hospitals,   where wimpled
nurses served   gray porridge

boiled stiff as   a handshake.
A rare snow   blocked 13
Dial Street—the   ambulance

could not pass.   No bombs that
evening. She   locked the door,
claiming the   only warm

room for her   self. Charlie
pounded from   the other side,
clutching two   blue infants

in dirty   nappies, but
she hurt too   badly to
hear them. Pain   divided

her. She pushed   with her palms
braced against   mildewed walls.
She pushed while   squatting next

to the deal   table. She pushed
on her hands   and knees and
the fairy   baby slid free,

smeared with blood   and vernix.
The ending   of one tale
and start of   another—

with gory   afterbirth
and a sick,   shuddering
cry. A hinge.

Bringing in the May, 1941

When the sirens cried,
my grandmother hustled four
babies into the mud-crowned
steel of the backyard shelter
and hooded them
by turning her back on the planes—
speck of grit in a wet city

The window glass blew
into the parlor
petals

No moving vans in blitzed
Liverpool, not even horses,
just white rubble strewn—
hawthorn branches—
she pushed the furniture
in a handcart through
the reborn streets

In the coal cellar of the new
house she sang of the bright
spring fires catching,
blossoming—
They trembled
as the morning light
trickled down in ribbons

Oh Aye Yeah, 1945

Her nana put seeds in everything she baked:
thyme in the cake, caraway in the bread,
tiny mouse spoor of poppy everywhere,
murder for a famished child to pick through.
No seed would infiltrate her, the girl vowed.
She swished her mouth with milky tea. Her country
was small and getting smaller, a model village
soon like Bekonscot roamed by giant princesses
in bobs and ankle socks, or a brief paved
garden plot with an outhouse, tin shelter
become a shed, and one unambitious swing.
And her father's voice was shrinking, all his stories,
the fairies languid on their wee couches.
The only growing thing was yes, once a rare
and brisk reply, now a surprised breath,
a cat's paw in a woman's conversation:
Oh, aye, yeah, I remember her, she died
when I was five, she would sigh one day.
She was little herself, her life twisted up hard
and bending her down, like the bun on her head.
Her long skirts caught fire. We knew she'd passed
the way me dad came home and walked straight up
the stairs without saying a word. Burnt seeds,
the girl thought, the opposite of flowers,
a pile of hopelessness swept into a pocket.

Gifts, 1946

She spent her weekly ration on dolly mix
because the pieces were small. She counted them out
and walked with her sacrifice to a grove

in Princes Park where oak and ash and thorn
grew together. Instead of saving the sweetness
for his tea, her father did the same:

cubes of sugar broken into granules,
carried in a matchbox while church bells scolded
through the mist. Let's not tell anyone.

Parents are inscrutable, their lives
all legend and anecdote. They start off as gods
but their power dwindles as fewer of us

believe in them. First you learn not to follow
the uncanny lights and soon you can't even spy
them anymore. A small brown shoe crunching

the moldy leaves. One grubby hand in her dad's,
the other clutching pastel-colored rolls,
jellies, foamy striped squares. Her nose

is leaking but she doesn't notice. He is telling
her not to stare too boldly—the people
need their peace—but he has glimpsed them, and

his mother did too, little folk flying on stems
of ragwort. Watch them this way, he says,
lowering himself onto one knee in the damp

and plucking a green spear. Bend it like so,
into a circle, and hold it next to your eye.
She believes. She understands mysteries.

The Residue, 1947

The bathwater, used three times, remembers
heat but does not feel it anymore. The tin tub
in the kitchen swallows the fourth child whole,
the little one who likes to watch the dirt float
from the grooves of his knees, the linty pockets
between his toes. Bubbles cluster in islands.

His mind is wordless but his stomach talks
to the apple-raisin pie cooling nearby. September,
you are a sad mood. The pie remembers summer,
warm and sweet, but does not feel it anymore.

His brother and his sisters are splendidly clean,
one head wetter than the next. Two play checkers
and one reads. Her pink legs are folded on the sofa
but they are also striding into a Concord Christmas,
strapped into ice skates or old-fashioned boots.

His mother says, sit forward now so I don't burn
you, and pours the fizzing kettle water in.
It smells of iron. Love swarms around him
in clouds, the way the smallest child is always
loved for his red cheeks and his sweet filth. He stretches
his back in it, dunks his head down, and her fingers
briskly dislodge the week from the roots of his hair.

All right, she says, out you go, and does not look
at his shivering. The tub must be dragged
to the garden, a whole month speckling the suds,
time washed away as it ought to be,
off their bodies, returned to the ground.

Otterspool, 1948

Ladies of the night, they whisper, winking.
American servicemen would ask us how
to find it—
the Cast Iron Shore, Cazzy for short. Here, kids,

have some chewing gum. The mint tasted
innocent, much fresher than the dusty
leaves that scent
our garden. We idled as the sun shifted.

This is where the rubbish goes—tipped
into the groynes between embankments. Soon,
landscaping,
a promenade laid down above the mess.

Once a fellow bribed us with cinnamon
candy. His watch flashed as he bent with a palm
full of sweets.
The secret burned our mouths. Ciphers. Blackout.

The Third Child Counts Her Options, 1949

We did own roller skates. I sometimes strapped
one over my shoe, gliding down Vronhill
Street like a sad flamingo. My sister

buzzed by on the other, pretending to
be a *Luftwaffe* raider. My brothers
rowed over the bicycle. There were four

of us, three fighters, and never enough
biscuits. One of us had to read the old
books instead. One of us had to sit still.

Sunday Afternoon in Liverpool, 1950

The aspirin at the heart of the jar.
The chipped-paint cupboard under the sink,
where mum keeps lye in a lemonade bottle.
The back of my hand in the rainy light.
Everything white has gone gray:
the chalk line down the middle of our bedroom floor,
the sheets Bobbie mussed to annoy me
before stalking off with the dog.
A family of six in a three-bedroom house—
I've scarcely known such a blank hour,
pure privacy gathering must. Fifth in line
for the crossword, I glare for a while
at the tangled chains four times erased,
yank the bow from my hair, sink into bed.
Gray. I know how to float away,
how to glance down at my lonely form
and, passing through walls dulled to mist,
fly to a world of heat and color,
Egypt sometimes, or just an English meadow.
One day I'll knock the coal soot from my shoes,
bleach my hair, and lift my body too.

Scholarship Girl, 1953

The scholarship girl paces to school
along broken pavements.
No one has cleaned the war up yet.
I swing my Shakespeare
against the wool on my hip,
my homemade blues.
Because I am tall,
I will play Caesar.

I will be smaller when I grow up.
Cockroaches will do their part.
I will study nursing
and go down to the laundry at night.
First I will tip the door open,
then stretch to reach the chain.
The light will reflect from a thousand
shiny carapaces scuttling away,
shrinking like a skirt in hot water,
lines forgotten suddenly.

But first there are rationed eggs,
and my sister calling *elephant eyes,*
and scholarship girls quarantined
in one crowded classroom.
Caesar's speeches will deflate
me one hot puff at a time
till I fit in anybody's pocket:
the starchy white one of the Sister
who docks my bus fare
in fine for laddered stockings,
or even yours. Listen
for my nails scratching
against the fabric.

Electrician's Mate, 1954

The steel pin coiled his arm like a filament
in a tungsten bulb. He had tumbled off
a scaffold while wiring neon signs. Now
he could not join the army, hold a gun.

*

The sky burned incandescent overhead.
He steered his family into the cellar,
leaned out with a hissing cigarette, watched,
counted the survivors under his breath.

*

Radium needles were inserted but
escaped, jutting through his skin. He wanted
to see rhododendrons flare awake,
not just the cage of his bed, his cancer.

*

You become your job and miss it more than
your wife, your children. Glass breaks but the current
is live. Anyone can see it leaping
in his eyes, searching for a way out.

Royal Liverpool Babies Hospital, 1956

Batty Batstone, seven months old, was dozing
in her pram, alone in the back of the garden,
dreaming of bees and lavender, when the rockets
     tumbled. Her people

all killed instantly. Herb in an untended
bed, she grew up spindly and short of bloom. In
nursing school she strived for spotlessness, shunning
     cigarettes, sweetness.

Other students mocked her for peeling oranges
in the bath, but nothing could stick to her. If she were
clean enough, the damaged babies would slumber
     safely in her hands.

The Dead Man, 1958

Home through the heart's forest after so
many little glasses of sherry, each sweet
as a headache, round and brown as an eye.

I've been dancing at the hospital again
with Paul. No father is waiting to chide me.
My mother is dead asleep.

When we miss the last bus together and trudge
down the middle of Aigburth Road
as if we're the only souls in the city,

we find the body, an ordinary man
shining in a suit and overcoat, no blood,
his hand a sliver of moon, one arm twisted

back, face down. It's a dangerous district. Sure
that we will meet a policeman, we both keep
hiking, but all the miles home we never do.

No kiss—Paul must find a phone. I hang up
my red macintosh. In the starry kitchen
I light the gas, boil water for tea

in the iron kettle, find bread under a cloth
and butter on the marble slab. He
was a fallen tree, hollow, our fears crawling

over his flesh. We hardly saw him.
The crumbs dissolve on my tongue
in distinct grains, butter slick and salt.

It takes a long time, learning something awful
but true. I pull my sister's shoes off.
They have rubbed raw spots on each heel,

the skin blistered and lifting off like haze
from the sun, two red-eyed suns. It's getting lighter.
The pain is a kind of warning and a kind of relief.

She Doesn't Remember the Beatles, 1961

A scholarship to forgetfulness, a room
where the windows look upward and the old sounds
dissolve, so much grime in a basin of water.

I might have heard The Quarrymen groove in some
cellar club—girls lowered themselves into
those mines all the time. And my mother
collected rumors on the installment plan
from Mrs. Starkey, who nattered on the street
all day in a dirty apron, boasting of Ringo's
schemes. Round and round the stories went.

They weren't famous and I didn't much care
for gormless boys making noise. Well,
I cared for one. He and his mates practiced
in the vacant flat next door, over the shop,
but he was a Catholic. Never scale those banks.
I spun the dial to a different song.

Sooty vinyl ribbed with ruts—plain
what kind of memories it stored.
I tuned all that steady pointedness,
diamond purpose, elsewhere, out, away.

Ten-Pound Pom Fails the Language Test, 1962

If you emigrate to Australia, you'll never
earn the fare to return, nor I to visit.
Might as well stop speaking to you now. Salt
          silence rushes in,

washes through the flat in wavelets. Mother and
daughter chill the air for a month with sea winds,
inarticulate. Distances ache. At last, one
          word: America.

Dressing Down, 1962

"Shalom," called the pink-shirted man in the Oceanic
Terminal of Heathrow, and I snapped,
"I do not want to talk to you." Manic

with fear, I extended one pointy-tipped shoe, tapped
the message home. My cases bulged with the wrong
clothes, every outfit trimmed with clipped

English, fit for telephone jobs on Long
Island. Rwanda, Algeria, and me
declaring every kind of independence.

My skirt and I were green, not the pretty
pistachio that Jacqueline Kennedy wore,
but the color copper develops in the sea,

cold and unfortunate, the green of storms
that have never squalled before. My hat,
gloves, and I were pale, not plush like the warm

blonde women settling in their seats
and bubbling dipthongs to their husbands;
not even poignant, like the champagne satin

that Marilyn Monroe was buried in.
Just neutral, stale as a biscuit, off
as an old cup of milk. I was stubborn,

I would do what I said and leave
England. I would ride that El Al jet, mystery
novel in hand, and never grieve.

Johnny Carson, the Jetsons, and me.
A new wardrobe in cartoon hues. Meanwhile,
my row-mate slipped off her court shoes, free

toes wiggling in hose. "We all went to Israel,
almost all of us on the flight, and are returning
to South Carolina," she explained in a drawl

that frightened me more that the turbofan
wailing beneath us. In her sundress, her stomach
looked soft. Ungirdled? Does everyone chat with a twang,

even the Jews? I do not want to talk,
but here I am, midair. "Coffee," I replied
to the hostess, slowly. I will never wear slacks,

but I can unfasten each word, open it wide.

The Forgetting Curve

Lazy Eye, 1978

The stranger unplugs her bogus teeth
with a damp pop, tossing discarded parts
across my room, where she bunks this summer.
She brings Cadbury bars and Oxo cubes.

I am ten and not Cassandra. The gods
broke me, didn't send a gift or a note—
Sorry, Second Sight *is out of stock.*
One eye glares at tomorrow, the other watches

the visitor. Off with the belt that cinches her fine
figure. She tucks her dress, as green as envy,
into the pastel sweetness of my closet.
A bra's silky cones protrude from her case.

I peel a scrap of plastic from one iris,
drop it in the shag, kneel to stroke
the rug, sit up to scrape the ball again:
could the lens still be drifting there? Have I lost

something, or not? Contacts improve me for other
lookers, but do not change what I see,
the double vision, partial views, the way
she's my grandmother, the way she's

a foreign country. *Oh, hyphenated you,*
the chorus mocks. I am a lucky girl, I have
souvenirs, I have plans, I can gaze along two
paths at once. Some kind of recompense.

Coalification, 1983

Shod in pink sandals,
free, she steps off the curb
and under a motorbike.

Six months oxidized
by regret. Her body shrinks
and alters. Each week

she cleans the ferns of
her hair with coal tar. Time, heat,
pressure wring her green

persistence down. What's
left is shut in rock: locked-up
force, a seam of fire.

Medical History, 1997

Four slits, one through my navel, the scope quick
as a snake. Our Lou, now, she had gallstones
for fifty years. At night she would ring
for the ambulance and when the pain
dissolved at dawn, she'd go home in a taxi.
My mum lingered too, after all those strokes.
Gone mean. Though everything hurts, the women survive.

Your granddad fell
from a scaffold at fifty.
Brain cancer twisted him.
He wouldn't speak to me.
His tenor, his fairy stories—
we used to walk to the pub
for beer and lemonade,
the empty jugs whistling.

The gallbladder is slight as a teaspoon,
your sister says, for all the bitterness
it hoards. She had hers out at twenty-two.
Never any patience for woe, that one.

Fresh Eggs

One day he tottered home stiff as a meringue.
A cargo ship had docked and, pretending
he had wiring to mend, the poor man shrugged
on an overcoat and sidled near the wharves.
His thin-faced children hadn't eaten eggs
since before the war. He jammed all his pockets
and walked miles home, but the shells slithered
down his skin, the whites churned into foam.
His beater legs set and cooked them. No one
could speak for laughing, him most of all,
when he finally arrived with the rain on his cheeks.

One grown daughter sits in a rose-lit kitchen
and peels them while they're hot. Too much love
to swallow. The hard-boiled velvet can choke
a person. Ornamental birdhouses hang
from her rafters, empty but for nests of yarn.
Her grandchildren glow with food and questions, as if
one breeds the other, tiny interrogatives
curled in the golden yolks. One asks how babies
are made. *Oh, eggs and seeds.* Wealth, or theft.

Theatrical Distances

Forty-odd years ago she packed five dollars,
a handkerchief, rode the train, bought
a matinee ticket to *The Fantasticks;*
Fiddler on the Roof; Hello, Dolly!;
one of the matchmaker musicals,
and sat down by herself. She did not want
to read the playbill. The sudden keen of tuned
strings should surprise a person, gilt
and velvet disappearing like a change
of mood, a taxi round the block.
In the audience, she knew, there is nothing
to worry about. Everything happened long
ago, in somebody else's heart.

I can't bear my own altitude over
the stage, the cynical gears and pulleys. I keep
thinking that it must hurt to be a flying
monkey, even more than it hurts to watch
them. They were changed by book enchantments
and a person who voiced a spell that she didn't
understand. I am changed by all
those fairy tales I heard—crying out
freakishly from above my sisters, sprouting
unnatural wings, so frightened, so elated.

Her Voice in My Mouth

There's a noise for grief I can't say or spell.
Her accent dispersed with the odor
of boiled cabbage: never quite.
For years she pronounced the *a*
in *mall* with the sound in *candle*,
flat as a pool of wax, while *tomato*
and *banana* melted into long sighs.

The vowels have quietly relocated,
whole phrases in consonantal drift.
She never steps into a Pennsylvania
July and says, *The sun's cracking the flags.*
My *greasy maulers* and *gravel rash*
have cleared up now. I feel them
as phantom limbs, like tea going cold
while I talk on the phone. The room
of my mouth remains full of ghosts.
Something is almost gone, a fume
of sound and all that it meant.

Megafauna

Yesterday's Camel, the Big-Headed
    Llama, and the Short-
        Faced Bear are almost
as extinct as our great-great-
    grandmothers—a jawbone
        here, a Latin name there,
a hand-me-down
    prosthetic. Random inheritance,
        inexplicable migrations.
Sometimes opportunistic
    herbivores attend barbeques
        in the wetlands, grazing on shrubs
and soggy New Jersey lawns.
    Wedgie sandals trample
        the glacial traces. Mega-
wine glasses brim with something
    fermented. Decrepit bulks withdraw
        into thickets when
the Saber-Tooth Cat flounces
    in late, her jewelry glittering.
        The next generation bounces
on the trampoline, beefing up
    for the end of the Pleistocene.
        The Giant Ground Sloths
on the deck might outweigh them
    presently, but smaller mammals will
        outwit the ice age, the hunters,
and us. Time now
    for the megavehicles to growl,
        to pack away the skeletons
and exhaust some fossil fuels. O
    bright furs and scales, how quickly
        the children will forget you. However,

plastic forks, swallowed surreptitiously
        by the springy ground, you will
                endure forever. The disposables
persist, the accidental
        print of a hoof in the mud,
                or your uncle's inexpensive
watch—the one we dropped into the tar
        pits while he had a smoke. The ticking
                was vulgar and made us feel old.

Oral Culture

In my classroom there are nine windows full of
        mountains, but eight of the windows are painted
        shut.
We mispronounce words on purpose and draw little
        marks over them, spears and cups and kisses.
In my classroom accent and sibilance, thump and stagger,
        chalk and analog.

I am paid to say formula, copia, and residue, and I am
        happy to say them, work and joy and religion.
My grandmother had a song for her name and a song for
        driving home and a song for childish love, but my
        children will not learn them.
My mother has a story for school clothes and a story for
        sherry and a story for wicked teachers, but my
        children want me to read to them from heavy
        books, the voices climbing up and down the scale,
        roughened by humors.

It is all good, pages and timbres, classrooms and mothers,
        but something is lost.
Or it is losing, loss of steam, loss of capital, loss of
        confidence, power.
I remember dialects changing as the blender whirred,
        suitcases emptied, suitcases packed.
Homemade ice cubes and powder for whisky sours. Not
        that people were kinder. They were bitter. The
        lemony foam flattened quickly, as if bubbles were
        more delicate then, thinner-walled.
Listen to the foam of my voice and I will pour it for you,
        all the tiny stories in one intoxicating stream,
        catching each other's sparkle,
now, before the taste disappears.

Born, We Didden Know We Was

There is no way to prove to you how
my mother's Liverpool sounded,
the slosh, the rattle of it, the catarrhal
schoolgirl recitations of "Daffodils"—

there is no grooved disk, no file
to click, no black-and-white child
to stand on the chair for a song

me auntie Mary had a canary
up the leg of her drawers

pulled down laughing into smoke
and the froth of Cain's Bitter,
slapped on the thigh, fled
to the garden with rope and chalk,

no poem croons Elvis or Ella
Fitzgerald on its cabinet radio,
the hiss of waves that will bear
the girls away, rinse from their minds

the liver birds crying. It's gone
for everyone and I was never
there with my spiral pad or

a microphone, the resonance
just caught in me, rain
in a lost shoe, grit in a pot
boiled often, rarely cleaned.

Most of my kin can't spell
or sing but they have gobs
like the Mersey tunnel, half blocked

by leaks and debris, half clear
for the charged traffic
of stories, and some of the dead
ones, they say, used to play

any instrument by ear.
I know something, a stain
your rags cannot wipe

off the paper: this place-and-time
was noisy once, and has a sound
still. No elegies here.

The Forgetting Curve

The first line on the graph falls almost plumb
with just a little forward kick at its base,
the kind a child makes one summer dusk,

her glossy brown head at rest against the rope
and the ball of one foot thrust once against the ground.
If a magpie lights on the garden wall, she might

look up, and the wind might pluck a fragrance
from a blossoming bough. The next line is stronger,
pulling against its knot at the top of the figure,

as if the child is pumping now, leaning in
and back again in the rhythm that makes a swing
travel. It teaches a girl that if she dips

into the past, over the weedy paving stones,
the leggy pansies dimming, she will rock
with corresponding force into the future.

The nineteenth-century Prussian who discovered
the exponential nature of forgetting
wrote that metaphors are insufficient

to the process of memory: beaten paths,
graven images. He proposed a formula,
sure that ideas endure, the way we infer

stars below the horizon—the universe
goes on even if we cannot see
it shine. He tested this by memorizing

poems. The girl on the swing wants to try
this hypothesis. Maybe the sky
looks different past this curve of the earth. Maybe

the stars are flowers torn from a branch—
suspended in the blue breeze as notes
on a staff, preserved until they can be sung.

Notes

"Heterotopia": The phrase "electric Afric hurrah" is from Allen Ginsberg's poem "Who Be Kind To." Section three refers to the 1896 film *Liverpool Docks;* Promio was a camera operator for the Lumière brothers. I base the definitions in section five on Michel Foucault's 1967 lecture, "Of Other Spaces."

"Mr. Hawthorne Peeks at Me Shelf Kit": Hawthorne served a term as U.S. Consul to Liverpool. "The Goose and the Gridiron" was a local nickname for the U.S. seal; a spirit-vault was a liquor store.

"Poem without a Landscape": "Scouse" can refer to the Liverpool accent or a thick stew of lamb and potatoes.

"The Calderstones": These reddish boulders, once part of a dolmen, now stand in Calderstones Park in Liverpool. "Judy" is scouse for "young woman" (sonnet 5). "Anny ur-gar, bols, buns" translates as "any rags, bottles, or bones" (sonnet 7). "The boy stood on the burning deck" is the first line of the poem "Casabianca" by Felicia Hemans, a poet born in Liverpool (sonnet 11).

"Bringing in the May, 1941": This refers both to May Day rituals and to the disastrous 1941 May Blitz on Merseyside.

"Gifts, 1946": "Dolly mixture" is a British candy assortment.

"Ten-Pound Pom Fails the Language Test, 1962": In the forties, Australia established a policy that subsidized immigration by Europeans in order to increase the country's white population. The reduced fare was ten pounds sterling.

"Born, We Didden Know We Was": The title is slang for "we were innocent." Wordsworth's poem "I Wandered Lonely as a Cloud" is often remembered as "Daffodils." To have a "gob like the Mersey tunnel" is to have a big mouth.

"The Forgetting Curve": Hermann Ebbinghaus created a formula in 1885 to demonstrate how memory declines over time. Depicted on a graph, the results are referred to as the forgetting curve.

Acknowledgments

I am grateful to the editors of the following journals, in which versions of these poems appear, sometimes other under different titles:

AGNI: "Forged"; "Scholarship Girl, 1953"
Barely South: "The Residue, 1947"
Barrow Street: "Heterotopia"
Blackbird: selections from "The Calderstones"; "Bringing in the May, 1941"; "Electrician's Mate, 1954"; "The Dead Man, 1958"
Elixir: "Poem without a Landscape"
The Journal: "Inland Song"; "Her Voice in My Mouth"
Kestrel: "Medical History, 1997"; "Theatrical Distances"
National Poetry Review: "Born, We Didden Know We Was"; "Lazy Eye, 1978"
Platte Valley Review: "Vronhill Street in Liverpool 8"
Poet Lore: "The Third Child Considers Her Options, 1949"
Poetry: "Dressing Down, 1962"
Slate: "Oral Culture"
Sou'wester: "Sunday Afternoon in Liverpool, 1950"
Spoon River Poetry Review: "Concerning the Līver Bird"

"Dressing Down, 1962" also appears in *Eating Her Wedding Dress: A Collection of Clothing Poems,* edited by Vasiliki Katsarou, Ruth O'Toole, and Ellen Foos (Ragged Sky Press, 2009). "Inland Song" and "Lazy Eye, 1978"were presented on *Verse Daily.* Some of these poems were published in the chapbook *Scholarship Girl* (Finishing Line Press, 2007).

Work on this manuscript was supported by Washington and Lee University's Glenn and Lenfest Grant programs and by a 2007-2008 Individual Artist Fellowship from the Virginia Commission for the Arts. I could not have written this book without the stories my extended family told, especially my mother and my grandmother, but also Tony, Bobbie, and Peter Cain and the McLeods. I am deeply grateful to David Wojahn, Peter Covino, and Talvikki

Ansel for their advice and encouragement, and to the many friends who read drafts, weighed titles with me, and buoyed my confidence in this project. Thanks most of all to Cameron, Madeleine, and Chris for inhabiting the heterotopias of composition and revision with me: I couldn't ask for better company.

Barrow Street Poetry

Heterotopia
Lesley Wheeler (2010)

This Noisy Egg
Nicole Walker (2010)

Black Leapt In
Chris Forhan (2009)

Boy with Flowers
Ely Shipley (2008)

Gold Star Road
Richard Hoffman (2007)

Hidden Sequel
Stan Sanvel Rubin (2006)

Annus Mirabilis
Sally Ball (2005)

A Hat on the Bed
Christine Scanlon (2004)

Hiatus
Evelyn Reilly (2004)

3.14159+
Lois Hirshkowitz (2004)

Selah
Joshua Corey (2003)